The Dangers of Spiritual Immaturity

Valy Vaduva
Author of *Fullness of Christ*

UPPER ROOM
FELLOWSHIP MINISTRY
Livonia, Michigan, USA

The Dangers of Spiritual Immaturity
© 2022 by Valy Vaduva

Published by Upper Room Fellowship Ministry (URFM)
Livonia, MI 48150
www.urfm.org

ISBN 978-1-930529-48-9 (sc)
ISBN TBD (E-book)
Library of Congress Control Number TBD

All rights reserved. No part of this book may be used or reproduced by any means, graphic, electronic, or mechanical, including photocopying, recording, taping, or by any information storage retrieval system without the author's written permission, except in the case of brief quotations embodied in critical articles and reviews.

This book is a work of non-fiction. Unless otherwise noted, the author and the publisher make no explicit guarantees as to the accuracy of the information contained in this book, and in some cases, the names of people and places have been altered to protect their privacy. The views expressed in this work are solely those of the author and do not necessarily reflect the opinions of the publisher.

Unless otherwise cited, scripture quotations are taken from the New American Standard Bible® (NASB), Copyright © 1960, 1962, 1963, 1968, 1971, 1972, 1973, 1975, 1977, 1995 by The Lockman Foundation. Used by permission.

Scripture quotations marked (CEV) are from the Contemporary English Version Copyright © 1991, 1992, 1995 by American Bible Society. Used by Permission.
The Good News Translation (2nd ed). 1992. New York: American Bible Society.
Scripture is taken from GOD'S WORD®, © 1995 God's Word to the Nations. Used by permission of Baker Publishing Group.

Because of the dynamic nature of the Internet, any web addresses or links contained in this book may have changed since publication and may no longer be valid. Cover design by Birdbrook Design.com).

Dedication

I dedicate this small book to all believers interested in discipleship and spiritual growth in Christ.

Contents

	Preface	i
	Prologue	1
1	Danger number one: *Carnality*	9
2	Danger number two: *Instability*	25
3	Danger number three: *Repulsion towards Solid Food*	29
4	Danger number four: *Spiritual Identity Ignorance*	38
5	I Danger number five: *Inability to Make a Meaningful Contribution to the Spiritual Body of Christ*	50
6	Spiritual Maturity: *Believers' Highest Priority*	65
	Upper Room Fellowship Ministry	84
	About the author	85

Preface

And I, brethren, could not speak to you as to spiritual men, but as to men of flesh, as to infants in Christ.
— 1 Corinthians 3:1

Therefore, leaving the elementary teaching about the Christ, let us press on to maturity, not laying again a foundation of repentance from dead works and of faith toward God.
— Hebrews 6:1

In the mid-90s, I was drawn by the Holy Spirit into the field of spiritual growth and maturity. At that time, I had a tiny "office" in the basement of our home. After work and after completing necessary chores, I would crawl into that office. Many times, I spent hours at a time digging into the Scriptures to learn more about this marvelous field. So, the thoughts and ideas I will share next have been springing up from Ephesians 4:11–16, a passage that has become very important to me over the years. I usually use this portion of Scripture to explain the importance of spiritual growth and maturity. However, during a mission trip to India and Italy a few years ago, I felt strongly led to start teaching and writing about the dangers of spiritual immaturity.

While in those foreign lands, it was a brand-new message for me too. I had never preached from this passage in this manner before. The message came freely from the depths of my heart without prior preparation. Before reading this chapter, I suggest you pause and pray for a few minutes:

> Father God, please open my eyes to see You, open my ears to hear the voice of the Spirit, open my heart and fill it with the love of Jesus, open my mind to comprehend the Scriptures, and empower me with the will to surrender my life one hundred percent to Your divine purposes. I pray in the wonderful name of Jesus Christ. Amen!

I have been praying for you, my readers, so I expect a deep understanding to come from above into your souls.

In Ephesians 4:11–16, Paul talks about the five-fold ministry of the church. I like to call it the *"hand"* of God. It contains the following *"fingers"*:

- Apostles
- Prophets
- Evangelists

- Pastors
- Teachers

This unique *hand* is given for the overall edification of the Body of Christ. All these unique *fingers* are called for a specific three-prong objective:

- For the equipping of the saints,
- For the work of service,
- To the building up of the body of Christ.

This objective was not finished during the apostolic generation of the Church in the first century. It continues today. I firmly believe that this great objective must be accomplished before the return of Christ. In this passage, Paul is saying that in the process of accomplishing this great tri-fold objective, three significant aspects must be kept in focus:

- Attaining to the unity of the faith and of the knowledge of the Son of God,
- Reaching the stature of a mature man, and
- Attaining the fullness of Christ" (see Ephesians 4:13).

It is my understanding that attaining the fullness of Christ is God's ultimate intention for His Church.

The *ultimate intention* of the church is a mature

disciple who knows God intimately and personally (cf. John 17:3), who accepted the discipleship call and carries the cross daily (cf. Luke 9:23; Galatians 2:20), whose mind and character are continuously renewed and transformed by the Spirit and the Word of God (cf. Romans 12:2; 2 Corinthians 3:18; Galatians 5:22–23), who grows and matures into the fullness of Christ (cf. Ephesians 4:11-16, Hebrew 5:11–14, 6:1-3), and who, ultimately, multiplies disciples according to the Christ's and the apostles' discipleship model (cf. Matthew 28:19– 20; 2 Timothy 2:2).[1]

This was the case for the first-century Church, which is still in effect for the Church of the last days before His glorious return. That is why I am passionate about writing about the *dangers of spiritual immaturity*. I am firmly convinced that these aspects are extremely important and urgent! If believers continue to remain in a state of spiritual immaturity, they are in danger of forfeiting God's purpose for their lives. Luke writes: "But the Pharisees and the lawyers rejected God's purpose for themselves, not having been baptized by John" (Luke 7:30). In other words, we can say: "But some Christians rejected God's purpose by not taking heed to their spiritual growth and maturity; therefore, they forfeited the ultimate intention of God for them."

In this portion of Scripture (Ephesians 4:11–16), Paul is not talking about salvation. Expounding upon this passage, I am not talking about salvation either. I am talking about the great danger of not reaching the full potential our loving Father desires for each of us as His beloved children.

Sadly, many Christians today are content with the *status quo*. So many churchgoers falsely believe that spiritual maturity is done on some *automatic pilot*. They think that just going through the motions will eventually result in growth, spiritual development, and maturity. This is precisely what the enemy of our souls would like us to think. But that doesn't lead to maturity.

Jesus warned us in the parable of the Sower. "The seed which fell among the thorns, these are the ones who have heard, and as they go on their way they are choked with worries and riches and pleasures of this life, and bring no fruit to maturity" (Luke 8:14). Even though the fullness of Christ is what the Father desires for all of us, it will not happen automatically.

Belonging to a local church does not cut it either. Spiritual growth and maturity are the result of spiritual transformation led by the Holy Spirit. As a result, God displays the life and character of Christ through the believer. Discipleship is factored in by our *intentions* and *decisions,* and our *faith* in *action* translates it out. It will not happen by itself. I believe that this is precisely what the Holy Spirit is speaking to churches today:

> *Believer, if you have an ear to hear, the will of the Father is to once again bring the cross of Christ to*

the forefront of the Church.

As the Holy Spirit impressed upon my heart, I perceived that there are five main dangers of spiritual immaturity. I invite you to investigate these dangers and decide accordingly.

May God bless you, my beloved!

Valy Vaduva

Endnotes

[1] Valy Vaduva, *Advanced Discipleship Training (ADT)*—Registration Manual, (Novi, MI, Upper Room Fellowship Ministry, 2010), 7.

Prologue

There is a lack of spiritual maturity in the North American church today. Nobody argues this anymore. Many Christian leaders agree that believers don't display the Life and the Character of Christ in and through them, even after many years of attending church services. Believers in North America have beautiful church buildings, many Bible translations, seminary-educated leaders, and access to much religious literature. However, despite all these excellent resources, believers lack spiritual maturity and transformation, leading to the *fullness of Christ*.

Years ago, Glenn McDonald, former Senior Pastor of Zionsville Presbyterian Church in suburban Indianapolis, considered that churches focused too much on the ABC (attendance, building, and cash) model, thus exhibiting at least two characteristics that prove to be „*disciple-making liabilities.*"

First, the tendency to look for programmatic solutions and opportunities. However, programs cannot and will not be acceptable substitutes for vision. God's vision for His church is disciple-making, not ABC or more programs.

Second, reliance on working hard and moving forward without really looking at the damage done to the case of Christ stated in Matthew 28:19–20.

McDonald writes:

> Classically, North American congregations have relied on a single individual to generate church-wide progress in bringing people to maturity in Christ. That person is the pastor. For roughly 300 years, Protestant pastors have been charged with the spiritual development of everyone within the church's reach—a mission to be accomplished through preaching, teaching, worship leadership, counseling, direction of appropriate boards and committees, home visitation, correspondence, administration, janitorial duties, praying at civic functions, and whatever other *"hats"* might be required apparel at a particular church. The ultimate issue, therefore, becomes: "How can we expose a maximum number of people to the work of our pastor so that he or she can work a maximum amount of spiritual magic?"[2]

This is an impossible task. I hope my readers see this too. Such a thing did not work, does not work, and will not work. Church leadership must return to the biblical principles of empowering the entire Body of Christ to grow, mature, and serve, as Paul stated in Ephesians 4:11–16.

Another important aspect is that many Christians don't see the need for spiritual maturity but instead feel content in a spiritually immature state (measured by Christian discipleship's biblical standard).

Jim Peterson writes:

> To be spiritual is to be dependent on the Spirit. This dependence should characterize our everyday relationship with Him . . . Maturity comes in time, out of a spiritual life that is nourished by increasing knowledge of Christ through experience with Him.[3]

I believe that this aspect is crucial and requires further explanation. Let's explore some critical reasons why spiritual maturity is ignored or resisted.

Firstly, there is a lack of knowledge. It is possible that many do not know the meaning of Christian and Christianity. Believers from almost any denomination take the word *Christian* lightly. It is possible that many don't even know that to be a Christian means to be a follower of Christ—a disciple of Jesus.

According to Professor Dallas Willard, the word "disciple" occurs 269 times in the New Testament. In contrast, the term "Christian" is found three times. Willard writes: *"The New Testament is a book about disciples, by disciples, and for disciples of Jesus Christ."*[4]

A disciple is a person who wants to be modeled and transformed by the Word of God through the power of the Holy Spirit from the inside out so she (or he), in character, heart, and will, looks more like Jesus Christ.

George Barna writes:

> Not one of the adults we interviewed said that their goal in life was to be a committed follower of Jesus Christ or to make disciples.[5]

What a tragedy! As Willard writes:

> The last command Jesus gave the church before he ascended to heaven was the Great Commission, the call for Christians to "make disciples of all the nations." But Christians have responded by making "Christians," not "disciples." This has been the church's Great Omission.[6]

Wow! It hurts my heart! But more than this, it breaks the heart of our Abba God.

Secondly, there is a superficial understanding regarding discipleship. It appears that most Christians consider it an unnecessary task.

The typical rejection is expressed like this:

> Since I am already saved, why should I waste my time with discipleship? I have recited the sinner's prayer and am on my way to heaven. Therefore, for that matter, I don't need discipleship or spiritual growth.

The Dangers of Spiritual Immaturity

George Barna writes:

> Most born-again adults have a very narrow view of what they are striving to become as Christians, what spiritual maturity might look like in their lives, and what it would take for them to maximize their potential as followers of Christ. The dilemma is not that believers deny the importance of spiritual growth or have failed to consider the challenges it raises, but that they seem to have settled for a very limited understanding of the Christian faith and their potential in Christ.[7]

I hope you see this difficulty, too, when it comes to discipleship and spiritual maturity. It is tough to ask believers to become disciples (Luke 9:23–24) when most churches don't insist on discipleship (Mathew 28:19–20) as part of their normal Christian life.

Thirdly, there is a superficial understanding regarding spiritual growth and maturity. The Scriptures clearly state that God desires His children to be different from the mainstream culture and to shine in this world. (See Matthew 5:14 and Philippians 2:15). But this requires our full engagement with the Spirit in the process of spiritual growth. (See 2 Corinthians 3:18, Romans 12:1–2).

Willard writes:

> Spiritual formation, without regard to any

specific religious context or tradition, is the process by which the human spirit or will is given a definite form or character. Make no mistake; it is a process that happens to everyone.[8]

The real question is, what type of character is it going to be? Willard continues:

Christian spiritual formation is the redemptive process of forming the inner human world so that it takes on the character of the inner being of Christ himself.[9]

This is exactly what God wants all His children to experience to the fullest measure possible. (See 2 Corinthians 3:18 and Ephesians 4:11–16).

The only hope many who call themselves Christians have, is to go to heaven when they die.

Barna writes:

The chief barrier to effective discipleship is not that people do not have the ability to become spiritually mature, but they lack the passion, perspective, priorities, and perseverance to develop their spiritual lives.[10]

I think that this is just depressing. No wonder Paul prayed so fervently for the church in Ephesus. Here is Paul's prayer:

> I pray that the eyes of your heart may be enlightened, so that you will know what is the hope of His calling, what are the riches of the glory of His inheritance in the saints, and what is the surpassing greatness of His power toward us who believe. These are in accordance with the working of the strength of His might which He brought about in Christ, when He raised Him from the dead and seated Him at His right hand in the heavenly places, far above all rule and authority and power and dominion, and every name that is named, not only in this age but also in the one to come. And He put all things in subjection under His feet and gave Him as head over all things to the church, which is His body, the fullness of Him who fills all in all. (Ephesians 1:17–23).

I am not sure about you, but as for me, I subscribe to Paul's prayer one hundred percent. Amen?

Endnotes

[2] Glenn McDonald, The Disciple Making Church: From Dry Bones to Vitality, (Faith Walk Publishing, Grand Rapids, MI, 2004), 7.

[3] Jim Peterson, Lifestyle Discipleship: The Challenge of Following Jesus in Today's World, (Colorado Springs, CO: Navpress, 1994), 132, 133.

[4] Dallas Willard, The Great Omission: Reclaiming the Essential Teachings on Discipleship, (New York, NY: Harper Collins Publishers, 2006), 3.

[5] Barna, George, Growing True Disciples: New Strategies for Producing Genuine Followers of Christ, (Colorado Springs, CO: WaterBrook Press, 2001), 6.

[6] Willard, (2006), front cover flap.

[7] Barna, 40, 42.

[8] Willard, 104.

[9] Willard, 105.

[10] Barna, 54.

-1-

Danger number one:
Carnality

Carnality is a very great danger of immaturity. In his first epistle to the Corinthians, Paul writes:

> And I, brethren, could not speak to you as to spiritual men, but as to men of flesh, as to infants in Christ. I gave you milk to drink, not solid food; for you were not yet able to receive it. Indeed, even now, you are not yet able, for you are still fleshly. For since there is jealousy and strife among you, are you not fleshly, and are you not walking like mere men? (1 Corinthians 3:1–3)

In the endnotes section, please see various renderings of these verses[11] from multiple Bible translations. First Corinthians 3:1–3 is a fascinating passage of Scripture. Paul uses different words to contrast and describe the spiritually immature state of the believers in Corinth.

These words are:

- Spiritual men
- Men of flesh
- As to infants in Christ
- Milk to drink
- Solid food
- Fleshly
- Jealousy
- Strife
- Mere men

It is essential to have a clear understanding of what these words really mean. The first expression used in this passage is *spiritual men*.

The term "spiritual," as used in the New Testament, indicates a person who has been regenerated, indwelt by Christ, enlightened by God, endued, and empowered by the Holy Spirit. They are conformed to the will of God, having the mind of Christ, and living a life led by the Spirit of God. The bottom line is that a spiritual person is a new creation born from above (cf. Romans 8:6; 1 Corinthians 2:15, 14:37; Colossians 1:9; 1 Peter 2:5). Spiritual men and women are committed followers of Jesus whom Christ indwells, and when a certain level of spiritual maturity is reached, these individuals display the Life and Character of Christ.

This type of person responded to the Gospel message (Romans 10:17) in faith (Ephesians 2:8–9) and with a repentant heart (Act 2:38), accepting Christ (Romans 10:9–10) as their personal Savior and Lord (Jude 1:25). Because of the redemption work (Romans 3:25) Jesus did on the Calvary cross (Colossians 1:20), through His blood (1 Peter 1:18–19), the Holy Spirit regenerated this person (John 3:3, 5–6) and brought them to spiritual life (Ephesians 2:4–5). This person was made a new creation in Christ (2 Corinthians 5:17), thus a *spiritual* person.

This marvelous work of grace is not for super-Christians. According to Galatians 3:28, it is for everybody, regardless of gender, race, social status, education, skin color, and so on. Please keep in mind that this is just the beginning. The work of grace does not stop at the spiritual birth event. The spiritual person continues in grace (2 Peter 3:18).

Spiritual men and women, at some point in their walk with Christ, accepted the call to discipleship (Matthew 16:24). By the Holy Spirit, they comprehended and experienced their co-crucifixion with Christ (Galatians 2:20). They understood their identity in the death (Romans 6:3), burial (Romans 6:4a), resurrection (Ephesians 2:6a), and ascension (Ephesians 2:6b) with Christ. Now, because of these active truths working in their lives, they gladly carry their cross daily (Luke 9:23) and willingly present their lives on God's altar as a genuine act of worship (Romans 12:1). They don't do these things to earn or keep their salvation.

Salvation is God's gift (2 Timothy 1:9). God is the only one who can preserve them. Since they are in Christ, nobody can snatch them from Christ's hand (John 10:28–29). Spiritual men and women do these things for the Kingdom's sake (Mathew 6:33), motivated by God's love (John 14:15), and out of reverence for Christ (Hebrew 12:28).

Spiritual men and women are actively part of spiritual growth (2 Peter 1:5–7), and God's work (Ephesians 2:10), for the benefit of others (2 Corinthians 12:15).

Please let me get a bit technical here and provide some definitions of the word *"spiritual."*

According to *Vine's Complete Expository Dictionary of the Old and New Testament Words*, the Greek word used in 1 Corinthians 3:1-3 is πνευματικός—pneumatikos. It corresponds to Strong's #4152. Pneumatikos: "always connotes the ideas of invisibility and of power." It does not occur in the Septuagint nor the Gospels. It is, in fact, an after-Pentecost word.

According to *Thayer's Greek Lexicon, Strong's New Testament* (Strong's #4152) πνευματικός—pneumatikos—has these meanings:

1. Relating to the human spirit, or rational soul, as the part of man which is akin to God and serves as his instrument or organ.
2. Belonging to a spirit, or a being higher than man but inferior to God, i.e., wicked spirits, Ephesians 6:12.

3. Belonging to the Divine Spirit;
a. in reference to things; emanating from the Divine Spirit, or exhibiting its effects and so its character.
b. in reference to persons; one who is filled with and governed by the Spirit of God (1 Corinthians 2:15). According to Galatians 5:16, 25, a spiritual man is one who walks by the Spirit and manifests the fruit of the Spirit in his own ways.[12]

Moreover:

According to the Scriptures, the *spiritual* state of the soul is normal for the believer, but to this state, all believers do not attain, nor when it is attained is it always maintained. Thus, the Apostle, in 1 Corinthians 3:1–3, suggests a contrast between this spiritual state and that of the babe in Christ, i.e., of the man who, because of immaturity and inexperience, has not yet reached spirituality, and that of the man who by permitting jealousy, and the strife to which jealousy always leads, has lost it. The spiritual state is reached by diligence in the Word of God and in prayer; it is maintained by obedience and self-judgment.[13]

The second phrase used here is *men of flesh*. Simply put, men of the flesh mean people controlled by their fleshly desires instead of by the Holy Spirit.

According to *Vine's Complete Expository Dictionary of the Old and New Testament Words,* the Greek word used here is σαρκικός—sarkikos. It corresponds to Strong's #4559. It derives from *sarx,* which means *flesh.*

Sarkikos signifies:

(a) "Having the nature of flesh," having its seat in the animal nature, or excited by it, as in 1 Peter 2:11. "Fleshly" or as the equivalent of "human," with the added idea of weakness. It also communicates the idea of un-spirituality, of human wisdom, "fleshly," as in 2 Corinthians 1:12.

Sarkikos also signifies:

(b) "pertaining to the flesh" (i.e., the body), as in Romans 15:27 and 1 Corinthians 9:11.[14]

Furthermore, the Greek word σάρκινος—*sarkinos—fleshly* corresponds to Strong's #4560. *Sarkinos* denotes:

"*Of the flesh, fleshly*" as in 2 Corinthians 3:3 KJV: "but in fleshy tables of the heart." "The adjectives "*fleshly,*" and "*carnal*" are contrasted with spiritual qualities in Romans 7:14; 1 Corinthians 3:1,3,4; 2 Corinthians 1:12; Colossians 2:18. Speaking broadly, the *carnal* denotes the sinful element in man's nature by reason of descent from Adam. On the other hand, the *spiritual* is that which comes by the regenerating operation of the Holy Spirit.[15]

The word *carnal* here σαρκινοις—sarkinois, is not the same word which is in 1 Corinthians 2:14, which is translated as "natural" ψυχικός—psuchikos. "That" refers to one who is unrenewed and who is wholly under the influence of his sensual or animal nature, and is nowhere applied to Christians.[16]

"The carnal state is a state of continual sinning and failure."[17] "Carnal Christians are persons under the influence of fleshly appetites, coveting and living for the things of this life."[18] Unfortunately, most believers in Corinth were in a carnal state.

According to *Gill's Exposition of the Entire Bible*:

> The carnal state Christians are not as unregenerate men are; but had carnal conceptions of things, were in carnal frames of soul, and walked in … a carnal conversation with each other; though they were not in the flesh, in a state of nature, yet the flesh was in them, and not only lusted against the Spirit, but was very predominant in them, and carried them captive so that they are denominated from it.[19]

Andrew Murray, in *The Master's Indwelling*,

writes: "In these carnal Corinthians, there was a little of God's Spirit, but the flesh predominated; the Spirit had not the rule of their whole life."[20]

Pastor J. B. Hall, in the "Carnal Christian" sermon, posted on sermoncentral.com, explains:

> The carnal Christian then, much like the lost person, serves to oppose the work of God in a church. He has his own agenda and is completely insensitive and unresponsive to the spiritual work God is trying to accomplish in His church.[21]

During my online research, when I typed the question, "What is a carnal Christian?" I got this answer:

> The key thing to understand is that while a Christian can be, for a time, carnal, a true Christian will not remain carnal for a lifetime.[22]

I like Andrew Murray's perspective on this subject:

> We shall say to Him, "*It must be changed. Have mercy upon us.*" But, ah! that prayer and that change cannot come until we have begun to see that there is a carnal root ruling in believers; they are living more after the flesh than the Spirit; they are yet carnal Christians.[23]

This angle is even more interesting! According to Andrew Murray, it is impossible for Christians to grow from the carnal state into the spiritual state. He considers it deception.

He writes:

> There are Christians who think that they must grow out of the carnal state into the spiritual state. You never can.[24]

Then what is the solution? He continues:

> What could help those carnal Corinthians? To give them milk could not help them, for milk was a proof they were in the wrong state. To give them meat would not help them, for they were unfit to eat it. What they needed was the knife of the surgeon. Paul says that the carnal life must be cut out. *"They that are Christ's have crucified the flesh"* (Gal. 5:24). When a man understands what that means and accepts it in the faith of what Christ can do, then one step can bring him from carnal to spiritual. One simple act of faith in the power of Christ's death, one act of surrender to the fellowship of Christ's death as the Holy Spirit can make it ours, will make it ours, will bring deliverance from the power of your efforts.[25]

Furthermore, Andrew Murray writes:

So, in the spiritual life, you may go to teacher after teacher, and say, *"Tell me about the spiritual life, the baptism of the Spirit, and holiness,"* and yet you may remain just where you were. Many of us would love to have sin taken away. Who loves to have a hasty temper? Who loves to have a proud disposition? Who loves to have a worldly heart? No one. We go to Christ to take it away, and He does not do it; and we ask, "Why will He not do it? I have prayed very earnestly." It is because you wanted Him to take away the ugly fruits while the poisonous root was to stay in you. You did not ask Him that the flesh should be nailed to His cross and that you should henceforth give up self entirely to the power of His Spirit. The key is in trusting and surrendering it to God.
It is the Holy Spirit alone who, by His indwelling, can make a spiritual man. Come then and cast yourself at God's feet with this one thought, "Lord, I give myself an empty vessel to be filled with Thy Spirit."[26]

The good news is that prayers like this receive a quick answer from the Father.

O, dear Father, I come before You with my empty vessel cleansed by the Blood of the Holy Lamb. "My God will fulfill His promise! I claim from Him the filling of the Holy Spirit to make me, instead of a carnal, a spiritual Christian.[27]

All these things sound so good on paper, don't they? But when the rubber meets the road, things appear to be different. The question is: Is there a genuinely spiritual life? Is such a thing possible for ordinary people like you and me? If it is: *How can you and I enter such a life?* Well, I am glad you have asked! Let me see if I can explain it in plain terms.

First, God is asking for it, and He promises this type of life. The Bible teaches: "Therefore you are to be perfect, as your heavenly Father is perfect" (Matthew 5:48). Jesus is telling us: "I came that they may have life, and have it abundantly" (John 10:10b).

Second, based on these two passages, it is clear that living this kind of life is impossible when believers try to live independently of God. Only Christ, through the Holy Spirit, operating in us, can live that kind of life. After all, it is His life.

So, what must we do? A few things are of vital importance:

- We must be *filled with the Spirit* (Ephesians 5:18),
- We must be *led by the Spirit* (Romans 8:14),
- We must *walk by the Spirit* (Galatians 5:25).

If we don't see these aspects clearly, we must repent. In other words, we must change our minds about carnality of any kind and see it as— incompatibility with God's nature of which we are partakers (2 Peter 1:4). It must be settled once and for all that for a genuine believer in Christ, these outbreaks of carnality should be an exception, not the rule.

Third, the believer must be convicted of the bankruptcy of their flesh. We must see something terribly wrong with our carnal state as believers and agonize before God to deliver us from it. Paul writes: "Wretched man that I am! Who will set me free from the body of this death?" (Romans 7:24). Without this deep conviction, we can never become truly spiritual men. Transitioning from the carnal to the spiritual state is one step away. At this point, we see Galatians 2:20 with a different set of eyes. We declare: "it is no longer I who live, but Christ lives in me." There must be a legal breakup with the flesh. And rest assured that the cross has done that (past tense). This is the place where Christ desires His brothers and sisters to live and operate, by Him and through Him. And this requires total surrender (Romans 12:1)—not just a one-time deal, but daily surrender, picking up and carrying the cross.

Spiritual and abundant life is a daily walk. It is a vibrant life, not a static one. Only in the position of total surrender can the Word of God renew the believer's mind. Only with the *renewal of the mind* (cf. Romans 12:2) and *transformation of character* (cf. 2 Corinthians 3:18) can the believer increasingly display the life and character of Christ, and thus be less and less carnal. As others may explain, this process is known as *progressive sanctification*.

If the Holy Spirit has convicted you about your

own spiritual state, I highly encourage you to declare before God three positive things:

- Father God, I desire to eat solid food. Please help me to grow.
- Dear Lord, I am so disappointed in how carnal I am because I am still clinging to the flesh. I realize now "that nothing good dwells in me, that is, in my flesh" (Romans 7:18). Take Your "knife" and cut it off.
- Dear Holy Spirit, assist me and guide me in the process of spiritual growth and maturity.

Now that you have made these powerful declarations let's pray to seal them at the heart level.

I am suggesting this prayer:

Oh, Abba Father, I know that You love me. I present before You my empty vessel cleansed by the pure Blood of Your Son, Jesus. I know that whoever comes to You will not be ashamed. I claim the filling of the Holy Spirit to make me a spiritual Christian instead of a carnal one. I pray in the wonderful name of Christ.

Endnotes

[11] Parallel Verses from various Bible Translations:
New International Version: Brothers and sisters, I could not address you as people who live by the Spirit but as people who are still worldly--mere infants in Christ.
New Living Translation: Dear brothers and sisters, when I was with you I couldn't talk to you as I would to spiritual people. I had to talk as though you belonged to this world or as though you were infants in the Christian life.
English Standard Version: But I, brothers, could not address you as spiritual people, but as people of the flesh, as infants in Christ. *New American Standard Bible:* And I, brethren, could not speak to you as to spiritual men, but as to men of flesh, as to infants in Christ.
King James Bible: And I, brethren, could not speak unto you as unto spiritual, but as unto carnal, even as unto babes in Christ. *Holman Christian Standard Bible:* Brothers, I was not able to speak to you as spiritual people but as people of the flesh, as babies in Christ.
International Standard Version: Brothers, I couldn't talk to you as spiritual people but as worldly people, as mere infants in the Messiah.
NET Bible: So, brothers and sisters, I could not speak to you as spiritual people, but instead as people of the flesh, as infants in Christ.
Aramaic Bible in Plain English: And I, my brethren, have not been able to speak with you as with spiritual ones but as with the carnal and as to babies in The Messiah.
GOD's WORD® Translation: Brothers and sisters, I couldn't talk to you as spiritual people but as people still influenced by your corrupt nature. You were infants in your faith in Christ.
Jubilee Bible 2000: And I, brothers, could not speak unto you as unto spiritual, but as unto carnal, even as unto babes in Christ. *King James 2000 Bible:* And I, brethren, could not speak unto you as unto spiritual, but as unto carnal, even as unto babes in Christ.
American King James Version: And I, brothers, could not speak to you as to spiritual, but as to carnal, even as to babes in Christ. *American Standard Version:* And I, brethren, could not speak unto you as unto spiritual, but as unto carnal, as unto babes in Christ.
Douay-Rheims Bible: And I, brethren, could not speak to you as unto spiritual, but as unto carnal. As unto little ones in Christ. *Darby Bible Translation:* And *I*, brethren, have not been able to speak to you as to spiritual, but as to fleshly; as to babes in Christ. *English Revised*

Version: And I, brethren, could not speak unto you as unto spiritual, but as unto carnal, as unto babes in Christ. *Webster's Bible Translation:* And I, brethren, could not speak to you as to spiritual, but as to carnal, even as to babes in Christ. *Weymouth New Testament*: And as for myself, brethren, I found it impossible to speak to you as spiritual men. It had to be as to worldlings—mere babes in Christ.
World English Bible: Brothers, I couldn't speak to you as to spiritual, but as to fleshly, as to babies in Christ.
Young's Literal Translation: And I, brethren, was not able to speak to you as to spiritual, but as to fleshly—as to babes in Christ.

[12] Pneumatikos. www.biblehub.com. Accessed on May 1, 2018. http://biblehub.com/ greek/4152.htm.

[13] W.E. Vine, Merrill F. Unger, William Whote, Jr., *Vine's Complete Expository Dictionary of the Old and New Testament Words,* (Nashville, TN, Tomas Nelson Publishers, 1996), 594-95.

[14] Sarkikos. www.studylight.org. Accessed on June 10, 2014. http://www.studylight.org/ dictionary/ved/view.cgi?n=411.

[15] Sarkinos. *Vine's Complete Expository Dictionary of the Old and New Testament Words*, 243.

[16] Sarkinois. www.studylight.org. Accessed on May 30, 2014. http://www.studylight.org/commentaries/bnb/view.cgi?bk=45&ch=3.

[17] Andrew Murray, *The Master's Indwelling,* 4. www.ccel.org. Accessed on June 12, 2014. http://www.ccel.org/ccel/murray/indwelling.html.

[18] "Carnal Christians," Adam Clarke Commentary on 1 Corinthians 3:1-3. www.studylight.org. Accessed on May 30, 2014. http://www.studylight.org/commentaries/acc/view.cgi?book=1co&chapter=003.

[19] "Carnal state Christians," Gill's Exposition of the Entire Bible, www.biblestudytools.com. Accessed on May 30, 2014. http://www.biblestudytools.com/ commentaries/gills-exposition-of-the-bible/1-corinthians-3-1. html.

[20] Murray, *Indwelling,* 5. www.ccel. Org. Accessed on June 12, 2014. http://www.ccel. org/ccel/murray/indwelling.html.

[21] J B Hall, "Carnal Christian," 5, May 30, 2008. www.sermoncentral.com. Accessed on May 30, 2014. http://www.sermoncentral.com/sermons/carnal-christian- j-b-hall-sermon-on-growth-in-christ-120681.asp?Page=1.

[22] "What is a carnal Christian?" www.gotquestions.org. Accessed on May 30, 2014. http:// www.gotquestions.org/carnal-Christian.html.

[23] Murray, *Indwelling,* 6.

[24] Ibid, 8.

[25] Ibid, 9.
[26] Ibid, 10.
[27] Ibid, 10.

-2-

Danger number two:
Instability

One of the most visible dangers of spiritual immaturity is *instability*. Paul writes: "As a result, we are no longer to be children, tossed here and there by waves and carried about by every wind of doctrine, by the trickery of men, by craftiness in deceitful scheming" (Ephesians 4:14). According to *Merriam Webster Dictionary*, "to toss," means to "to throw (something) with a quick, light motion, to move or lift quickly or suddenly, to move (something) back and forth or up and down."[28]

Paul uses four words to warn believers about the danger of spiritual immaturity:

- Trickery
- Craftiness
- Deceitful
- Scheming

The word *trickery* in this verse refers to the opposite of being honest, truthful, frank, and open. According to Merriam-Webster Dictionary, the word craftiness is "the skill in achieving one's ends through indirect, subtle, or underhanded means."[29]

Deceitful means to do something based on or using dishonest methods to acquire something of value.

The fourth word used by Paul is *scheming,* which means being clever at attaining one's ends by indirect and often deceptive means.

Paul is not using this combination of words to impress the believers in Ephesus with his elevated Greek vocabulary. Under the inspiration of the Holy Spirit, Paul wanted to emphasize the danger of instability when believers remain in a childlike state. In other words, if we don't want to be carried about by every wind of doctrine, we must grow up in the knowledge and grace of Christ.

Immature believers do not have a stable theological stand. If a preacher says something, they are moved in that direction. If a different teacher comes in and preaches something else, they are thrown in that direction. Without spiritual maturity, believers are in danger of being carried away by the *trickery of men*. Deceitful men win over people who are carried about with ease. These men have some false *charisma* to gain the sympathy of their audience. The bottom line is that immaturity, a childlike state, is dangerous because of instability.

If this describes you, then please acknowledge this

danger in your life. I am asking you to declare three positive things:

- God, I need stability.
- Lord Jesus, I have decided to grow.
- Holy Spirit, please make me stable and consistent in my faith and walk with You.

After making these necessary declarations, I encourage you to kneel before God and pray this prayer:

Father God, I want to be stable. I have decided to embrace the process of spiritual growth and maturity. Dear Lord Jesus, I realize that growing and maturing in Your knowledge and grace is the only way I can be stable. Precious Holy Spirit, please work in me, transform me, and develop me according to God's plans and purposes. My only desire is to display the Life and the Character of Christ. I pray in the name of Jesus. Amen.

Endnotes

[28] To toss. www.merriam- webster.com. Accessed on April 23, 2014. http://www.merriam- webster.com/dictionary/tossed.

[29] Craftiness. www.merriam- webster.com. Accessed on May 29, 2014, http://www.merriam- webster.com/thesaurus/craftiness.

-3-

Danger number three:
Repulsion towards Solid Food

Spiritually speaking, *milk* stands for the "elementary teaching about Christ." According to Hebrews 6:1-2, *the milk diet* includes teachings about "repentance from dead works," teachings about "faith towards God," teachings about Church Sacraments, "resurrection of the dead and eternal judgment."

Milk is good! No question about it. But milk is the primary food for babies, not for adults. As any good parent, our Father does not want His children to continue indefinitely on the milk diet. God desires us to "grow in respect to salvation," as Peter puts it so well in 1 Peter 2:1–3. For this to happen, we must "press on to maturity" (Hebrews 6:1), which requires a willful decision. Pressing on is not an easy task; it implies overcoming resistance; it requires stick-to-itness.

Moreover, pressing on requires advancing, heading toward, making headway, and progressing. As you can see, all these words suggest something dynamic, not static.

Solid food stands for advanced teaching regarding the righteousness of God and spiritual discernment.

According to 2 Peter 3:18, solid food refers to mature teaching about the grace and knowledge of Christ.

According to Paul's prayers in Ephesians 1:15–23 and 3:14–21, solid food means an enlightened understanding of our identity in Christ and a deep comprehension of agape love and its spiritual dimensions.

Based on Paul's teaching in Romans 8:14 and Galatians 5:16–26, solid food represents a correct understanding of what it really means to be led by the Holy Spirit.

Moreover, solid food implies a deep knowledge of what it means to be transformed into Christlikeness (2 Corinthians 3:18; 1 Corinthians 5:2–3).

Immature believers have a *natural* tendency to dislike solid food. Repulsion is a feeling of intense dislike or disgust towards something.

D. A. Carson writes:

> But there are Christians who are international-class projectile vomiters, spiritually speaking, after years and years of life. They simply cannot digest what Paul calls "solid food." You

must give them milk, for they are not ready for anything more. And if you try to give them anything other than milk, they upchuck and make a mess of everyone and everything around them. At some point, the number of years they have been Christians leads you to expect some mature behavior from them, but they prove disappointing. They are infants still and display their wretched immaturity even the way that they complain if you give them more than milk. Not for them solid knowledge of Scripture, not for them mature theological reflection; not for them growing and perceptive Christian thought.

They want nothing more than another round of choruses and a "simple message"—something that won't challenge them to think, to examine their lives, to make choices, and to grow in their knowledge and adoration of the living God. So, the Corinthians, then, are wretchedly immature believers.[30]

In my travels around the world teaching about spiritual growth and maturity, I heard so many excuses (even from Christian leaders) regarding spiritual growth. Let me share just a few of them:

- It is so hard! Even the Bible in Ecclesiastes 12:12 tells us that too much teaching is weary to the body.

- I do not want to acquire too much knowledge because God will expect much from me. (See Luke 12:48).
- I don't have to study the Bible before I preach or make myself a plan or a sermon sketch because the Holy Spirit will give me the exact words I must speak. (See Mark 13:11).
- It is written not to have too many teachers. (See James 3:1).

If you look at the Bible references, I provided, all these Scriptures are taken out of context, proving further the danger of spiritual immaturity.

Obviously, a biological baby cannot be transitioned overnight from *milk* to *solid food*. It would be foolish to have such unrealistic expectations. It is a gradual process. They must be weaned first.

The taste buds of a baby must be cultivated to *like* solid food. In the same way, our spiritual "taste buds" must be cultivated to desire solid food over some time. But by no means should the weaning period take forty years; perhaps three or four, but not more than that.

Charles R. Swindoll writes:

You see, in order for a Christian to handle solid food, he has to have a grown, mature digestive system. He needs teeth. He needs to have an appetite that is cultivated over a period of time for deep things, for the solid things of God. Spiritual babies must grow up. Some of the most difficult people to live with in the church of Jesus Christ are those who have grown old in the Lord but haven't grown up in Him.[31]

The more we delay our exposure to solid food, the longer it takes to like it. It requires a willful decision to move from milk to solid food; otherwise, we will remain "dull of hearing."

The author of Hebrews puts it this way: "But solid food is for the mature, who because of practice have their senses trained to discern good and evil" (Hebrews 5:14).

You probably noticed this already, but assessing spiritual maturity is difficult. Many believers erroneously assume that they will automatically mature spiritually as time passes.

Unlike physical maturity, which is primarily a function of time, spiritual maturity is not. The time factor is obvious when it comes to physical maturity. We can easily differentiate between a three-year-old boy and a thirty-year-old man.

In the spiritual realm, growth and maturity are not a function of time but rather a function of our spiritual diet. For example, some Christians out there could have been attending the local church for thirty years and still be at the level of a toddler, acting like a three-year-old Christian. With proper discipleship, it is possible for a Christian who received Christ three years ago to be spiritually mature, displaying the life and character of Christ. (See Galatians 5:22–23; John 15:8).

Spiritual immaturity affects our speech, thinking, and decision-making. Paul writes: "When I was a child, I used to speak like a child, think like a child, reason like a child" (1 Corinthians 13:11a). Therefore, it is imperative to engage in the process of spiritual growth and maturity immediately so we can do away with childish things. Paul continues: "when I became a man, I did away with childish things" (1 Corinthians 13:11b).

The opposite of immaturity, of course, is spiritual maturity. Maturity is the high calling of every child of God, and one's priorities primarily evidence it. Do we continue to pursue the *things* and *success* of this world or seek the goal of God set before us—*Christ?*

Paul writes: "I press on toward the goal for the prize of the upward call of God in Christ Jesus" (Philippians 3:14). If the great apostle Paul felt the need to "press on," how much more you and I must do it?

Paul admonishes Christians engaged in the process of perfection with these words: "Let us, therefore, as many as are perfect, have this attitude; and if in anything you have a different attitude, God will reveal that also to you" (Philippians 3:15).

Christian maturity does not mean sinless perfection. It does not mean that mature people are of a higher class than individuals who cannot humble themselves to live in unity with others. By no means!

The Greek word *perfection* (Gr. τέλειος, teleios)[32] used by Paul in Philippians 3:15 means:

> Full age, adulthood, full-grown, of persons, meaning full-grown in mind and understanding (cf. 1 Corinthians 14:20); in the knowledge of the truth (cf. 1 Corinthians 2:6; Philippians 3:15, Hebrews 5:14); in Christian faith and virtue (cf. Ephesians 4:13).[33]

Paul explains: "However, let us keep living by that same standard to which we have attained" (Philippians 3:16). As Meldenius Rupertus a German Protestant theologian of the 17th century (aka Peter Meiderlin) once said: "In essential unity, in non-essential liberty, in all things charity."[34]

Spiritual maturity is not a competition between who can recite more theological facts. Instead, spiritual maturity is evidenced by love—*agape love*.

The Bible teaches us: "But the goal of our instruction is *love* from a pure heart and a good conscience and a sincere faith" (1 Timothy 1:5). In other words, genuine spiritual maturity is characterized by displaying a genuine and mature agape love, which is the very nature of God.

Believe me, it was not pleasant to write this chapter, and I am sure it was not pleasant for you to read it, either. Please, do yourself a great favor, and declare before God three positive things:

- God, I am hungry for solid food.

- Holy Spirit, I desire to eat like a mature Christian.
- Dear Lord Jesus, I am in pursuit of spiritual growth. My deep desire is to be a mature Christian. I invite You to display the life and character of Christ in me.

Now that you have declared these critical statements, please seal them in a prayer like this:

Dear God, please plant a deep desire for Your Word in me. Please develop my taste buds for solid food. O, Lord Jesus, please carry me in Your arms and take me to green pastures so I can grow more and more into Your grace and knowledge. So, help me, God. Amen!

The Dangers of Spiritual Immaturity

Endnotes

[30] D. A. Carson, *The Cross and Christian Ministry*, (Grand Rapids, MI: Baker Books, 2004), 72.

[31] Charles R. Swindoll, *The Tale of the Tardy Oxcart*, (Nashville, TN: Word Publishing, 1998), 80.

[32] 1τέλειος, (teleios): Short Definition: perfect, full-grown, perfect, (a) complete in all its parts, (b) full grown, of full age, (c) especially of the completeness of Christian character. www.biblehub.com. Accessed on August 11, 2014. http://biblehub.com/greek/5046.htm.

[33] Spiros Zodiathes, *The Complete Word Study Dictionary: New Testament,* (AMG International, Chattanooga, TN: 37422, 1993), 1372.

[34] "A common quotation from "Augustine"?" Posted by Steve Perisho. www.faculty.georgetown.edu. Accessed on February 6, 2024. https://bit.ly/3SwJgAE.

-4-

Danger number four:
Spiritual Identity Ignorance

What a tragedy to be a child of God and yet still be ignorant about your spiritual identity. If Christians only see themselves as *sinners saved by grace,* they have a view that is highly detrimental to their core identity. Immature believers cannot comprehend who they are in Christ. They don't understand that they are already righteous in God's sight. As God's children, we have access to all that God has. Due to immaturity, practically speaking, we cannot possess His riches yet.

Let me illustrate this point. While slaves in Egypt, God promised the Jews a country flowing with milk and honey—the Promised Land.

God told Moses:

> So, I have come down to deliver them from the power of the Egyptians, and to bring them up

from that land to a good and spacious land, to a land flowing with milk and honey, to the place of the Canaanite and the Hittite and the Amorite and the Perizzite and the Hivite and the Jebusite. (Exodus 3:8)

At least 600,000 adult-male Jews received this promise from God. This was a glorious offer. As we all know, God cannot lie (cf. Hebrews 6:18). Still, because of their unbelief, which, according to Hebrew 3:17–19, leads to disobedience, only two of them entered the "land flowing with milk and honey." This represents only 0.00033% of the Jews who received the promise. I think that this is heartbreaking for the heavenly Father. Spiritual immaturity is dangerous and costly.

Paul writes:

Now I say, as long as the heir is a *child* (Gr. νήπιος, népios[35]), he does not differ at all from a *slave*[36] although he is the owner of everything. (Galatians 4:1)

The person who lacks maturity cannot speak spiritual thoughts using spiritual words because they are unlearned and unenlightened (1 Corinthians 2:13–14). Therefore, they cannot handle the spiritual inheritance of God. As a result, the Father cannot entrust them with anything of importance.

As God's children, we have been seated with "Him in the heavenly places in Christ Jesus"

(Ephesians 2:6). By spiritual birth, this is our rightful position. However, without developing "wings" through spiritual maturity, we cannot fly like eagles; instead, we keep gobbling the same words as turkeys going around and around the same old barn.

To receive and handle spiritual responsibilities, God's children are required to grow and mature in "the grace and knowledge of Christ" (2 Peter 3:18). For us to leave the spiritual poverty of the old "barn," we need to grow wings like eagles and fly higher in the sky.

The author of Hebrew writes so boldly about this: "For everyone who partakes only of milk is not accustomed to the word of righteousness, for he is an infant" (Hebrews 5:13). Therefore, when it comes to spiritual identity, the doctrine of the believer's righteousness is crucial.

Righteousness is the state of moral perfection required by God to enter heaven. Dikaiosuné, [37] which means righteousness, "is the thus conformity to the claims of higher authority and stands in opposition to anomia (Strong Number 458), lawlessness."

According to *Merriam-Webster Dictionary*, to be righteous means: "Acting in accord with divine or moral law: free from guilt or sin."[38] Fairness, goodness, honor, justness, rectitude, respectability, uprightness, and virtue are synonyms for righteousness.[39]

The entire Old Testament Law, including the Ten Commandments plus the "moral" Law which, according to some Old Testament experts, amounts to approximately 613 laws, represents the moral character of God. The "Law is holy, and the commandment is holy and righteous and good" (Romans 7:12). But when it comes to conferring us His righteousness, because of the flesh, the Law is impotent (Romans 8:4). The New Testament teaching is clear that "by the works of the Law no flesh will be justified" (Galatians 2:16).

To make sure I am not taking it out of context, I would like to say a few things about the Law.

- First, the role of the Law was to show how horrible sin is. Paul explains "that through the commandment (Law) sin would become utterly sinful" (Romans 7:13).
- Second, the Law was just a tutor for us, to direct us to Christ. The Bible says, "Therefore the Law has become our tutor to lead us to Christ, so that we may be justified by faith" (Galatians 3:24).

The Scripture makes it clear that when Christ came, there was no longer a need to remain under this "tutor." "But now that faith has come, we are no longer under a tutor" (Galatians 3:25).

When it comes to the theme of righteousness, Paul sets the record straight. He teaches that we "may be found in Him, not having a righteousness of my own derived from the Law, but that which is through faith in Christ, the righteousness which comes from

God on the basis of faith" (Philippians 3:9).

According to the New Testament, the foundation for our righteousness as New Covenant believers is solely based on the finished work of Christ on Calvary's Cross—His death, resurrection, and His ascension.

A New Testament believer is considered righteous by faith in Jesus Christ (see Romans 4 and 5). More profoundly, righteousness is more than being right with God. The Bible teaches that our righteousness is Christ Jesus Himself who dwells in our hearts (see Philippians 1:20–21, Romans 8:10, 1 Corinthians 1:30, Galatians 2:20, Ephesians 3:17, Colossians 3:4).

Moreover, in his prophetic writings, Jeremiah speaks about Messiah as "a righteous Branch" (Jeremiah 23:5) and that He will be called "The LORD our righteousness" (Jeremiah 23:6). This was prophesied several hundred years before the crucifixion of Christ! No wonder Paul writes so confidently that Jesus Christ is our righteousness: "But by His doing you are in Christ Jesus, who became to us wisdom from God, and righteousness and sanctification, and redemption" (1 Corinthians 1:30). Regarding righteousness, 1 Corinthians 1:30 is one of my all-time favorite verses. Also, 2 Corinthians 5:21 spells it out very clearly: "He (God) made Him who knew no sin to be sin on our behalf so that we might become the righteousness of God in Him." According to this verse, as God's children, we have righteousness as valuable and precious as Christ's righteousness. Why? Because He is our righteousness.

The basis of our salvation and the only hope for righteousness stands firm on:

> (a) Christ's blood on Calvary (see Romans 4:25, 5:9, 8:3–4, 1 Corinthians 15:3, Galatians 2:20, Ephesians 1:7, Hebrews 9:14, 1, Peter 1:18–19, 1 John 4:10), and
> (b) His resurrected life in our hearts (see: Romans 4:25, 5:9-10; 8:10–11, Galatians 2:20, Colossians 3:1–3).

Paul is the expert in the doctrine of righteousness. He argues and demonstrates this vital topic from multiple angles. The first part of Romans is dedicated to receiving righteousness by faith. He writes: "For in it (the Gospel) the righteousness of God is revealed from faith to faith; as it is written: "But the righteous man shall live by faith" (Romans 1:17).

Then in Romans 3:21–22, we read:

> But now apart from the Law the righteousness of God has been manifested, being witnessed by the Law and the Prophets, even the righteousness of God through faith in Jesus Christ for all those who believe; for there is no distinction.

Secondly, Paul does not say anywhere in the New Testament that righteousness is obtained by observing the Old Testament Law. He writes: "Because by the works of the Law no flesh will be justified in His sight" (Romans 3:20). Even the righteousness Abraham received, he received by faith.

Paul writes:

> For what does the Scripture say? Abraham believed in God, and it was credited to him as righteousness... But to the one who does not work, but believes in Him who justifies the ungodly, his faith is credited as righteousness. (Romans 4:3, 5)

> Otherwise, it would be based on merit, and the promise would be invalidated: "For if those who are of the Law are heirs, faith is made void, and the promise is nullified. (Romans 4:14)

Some may ask: "Brother Valy, are you suggesting that since we have Christ's righteousness, it does not matter how we conduct our lives?" May it never be! This is a big misunderstanding. Paul was misunderstood as well.

Remember how he responded to this kind of question: "What shall we say then? Are we to continue in sin so that grace may increase?" (Romans 6:1). He answered his rhetorical question: "May it never be! How shall we who died to sin still live in it?" (Romans 6:2).

To be righteous at the inner core of our beings

and continue in sin is incompatible. It is like going against our very nature.

Let me try to illustrate it for you. A lion is a carnivore. It is in his nature to eat meat. A cow is an herbivore. It is in her nature to eat grass. For a lion to eat grass would be against his very nature. For a cow to eat meat would be against her very nature. For a Christian to continue in sin would be incompatible with their very nature—a saint and partaker of God's nature.

Does all this mean that God is not interested in moral behavior or in character development just because we have Christ's righteousness? Of course not. This is a deception coming from the pit of hell. God is very interested in our behavior, but He does not grant us His righteousness based on our changed behavior. This would mean re-instituting the Old Testament Law.

So how did God get around this? In Christ, God crucified us also and then resurrected us in Him, thus making us as righteous as Christ. God placed us in Christ, and when Christ died on the cross, we died with Him (cf. Romans 6:3–4); when He was raised from the dead, we were raised with Him (Colossians 2:12); when He ascended to the right hand of the Father we were (past tense) also seated with Him at the right hand of the Father in Christ (Ephesians 1:12, 2:6). Pretty awesome!

Now, because of our position in Christ and since He is in us (Colossians 1:27), sin no longer has dominion over us, so we can freely live for God. It appears simple, but it is not simplistic. The Bible teaches us: "Present yourselves to God as those alive from the dead, and your members as instruments of righteousness to God" (Romans 6:13).

Since we are not under the Law, but under grace (cf. Romans 6:14), we continue to be saved by Christ's life. Paul writes: "For if while we were enemies we were reconciled to God through the death of His Son, much more, having been reconciled, we shall be saved by His life" (Romans 5:10).

The secret of living a victorious and fulfilled life is *Christ's life*. Because Christ indwells us, we can present ourselves and all our members to God in obedience, and, as a result, we enjoy practical righteousness. The Bible tells us: "Do you not know that when you present yourselves to someone as slaves for obedience, you are slaves of the one whom you obey, either of sin resulting in death, or of obedience resulting in righteousness?" (Romans 6:16). Now, because of our special position *in Christ*, we became slaves of righteousness (cf. Romans 6:18).

Is God interested in holiness? Of course, He is. His standards of holiness have not changed, not even by one micron[40]. More than that, God is looking for genuine holiness. How can Christians attain it? Only in one way—by presenting ourselves and our members as slaves to righteousness. This will result in sanctification.

Please make a note and keep it handy: *This is the*

only way Christians arrive at genuine holiness. Yes, (cf. Matthew 22:11-12) Christians are required to be holy people. But make sure this is read in the context of Revelation 19:7-8.

Does this mean that salvation is by faith and sanctification by works? Of course not! This is the enemy's trap to cause us to act independently from God. This is living and walking after the flesh. Paul strongly rebukes this way of thinking and acting. He writes: "Are you so foolish? Having begun by the Spirit, are you now being perfected by the flesh?" (Galatians 3:3).

"Brother Valy, I am confused!" some may exclaim. Do you mean I cross my arms over my chest and do nothing? Am I being perfected by some automatic pilot? No. Not at all. The Bible teaches us that we have an active role in the process of progressive sanctification. Paul explains: "So then, my beloved, just as you have always obeyed, not as in my presence only, but now much more in my absence, work out your salvation with fear and trembling" (Philippians 2:12).

Some may say: *"Well… that sounds like "work" to me."* It may sound like that, but it isn't. In God's economy, the power source and motivation make all the difference. Paul is saying to *work out our salvation*, **not to work for our salvation**. The following verse explains it: "For it is God who is at work in you, both to will and to work for His good pleasure" (Philippians 2:13). In the end, what counts is Christ's life being manifested in and through us.

Furthermore, Paul writes: "When Christ, who is our life, is revealed, then you also will be revealed with Him in glory" (Colossians 3:4). That is why knowing who we are in Christ is an essential key to spiritual victory. Therefore, when it comes to the theme of our spiritual identity, we must be honest with ourselves; otherwise, it will cost us dearly.

With a much fuller understanding now, let's declare before God three positive things:

- God, I am so ignorant of who I really am.
- Dear Lord Jesus, I want to grow into my rightful position as a mature son (huios) and thrive in God's household.
- Holy Spirit, please reveal to me my spiritual identity.

Now let's bow before God in prayer with these words:

Father God, I thank you for placing me in Christ, so I died with Him when He died on the cross. I believe with all my heart that when You raised Jesus from the dead, You also justified me and made me righteous in Him. I have no words to thank You for the glorious position of being seated with Christ at Your right hand in heaven. This is my identity, my destiny; this is my new life now. I am the righteousness of God in Christ. I pray in the wonderful name of Jesus, Who is my life, my everything. Amen.

The Dangers of Spiritual Immaturity

Endnotes

[35] Spiros Zodiathes, *The Complete Word Study Dictionary: New Testament*, (AMG International, Chattanooga, TN, 37422), 1993 νήπιος, népios – Strong number 3516: One who cannot speak, hence, an infant, child, baby without any definite limitation of age. By implication, a minor, one not yet of age (as in Gal. 4:1). Generally, in the Septuagint, used of a child playing in the streets (as in Jer. 6:11; 9:21); asking for bread (as in Lam. 4:4). Metaphorically a babe, one unlearned, unenlightened, simple, innocent (as in Matt. 11:25, Luke 10:21, Rom. 2:20). Implying censure (as 1 Cor. 3:1; Gal. 4:3; Eph. 4:14; Heb. 5:13). Synonyms teknon—Strong number 5043: child, newborn child, infant. Antonyms: huios: Strong number 5207: a mature son or daughter.

[36] δοῦλος, doúlos – Strong number 1401: someone who belongs to another; a bond-slave, without any ownership rights of their own. www.biblehub.com. Accessed on August 11, 2014. http://biblehub.com/greek/1401. htm.

[37] δικαιοσύνη, dikaiosuné – Strong number 1343: righteousness: "divine approval," "God's judicial approval." "Deemed right by the Lord (after His examination)," "what is approved in His eyes." www.biblehub.com. Accessed on May 1, 2018. http://biblehub.com/greek/1343.htm

[38] Righteous. www.merriam- webster.com. Accessed on January 24, 2013. http://www.merriam- webster.com/dictionary/righteous.

[39] Righteous. www.thesaurus.com. Accessed on January 24, 2013, http://thesaurus.com/browse/righteousness.

[40] One micron is one-millionth of a meter. There are 25400 microns in one inch. The eye can see particles to about 40 microns. www.engineeringtoolbox.com. Accessed on August 12, 2014. http://www.engineeringtoolbox. com/particle-sizes-d_934.html.

-5-

Danger number five:
Inability to Make a Meaningful Contribution to the Spiritual Body of Christ

Paul writes:

> But speaking the truth in love; we are to grow up in all aspects into Him who is the head, even Christ, from whom the whole body, being *fitted* and *held* together by what *every joint* supplies, according to the proper working of each individual part, causes the growth of the body for the building up of itself in love" (Ephesians 4:15–16).

It is vitally important to understand that God is looking at both the spiritual growth and maturity of the individual member and the growth of the entire body.

- First: "We are to grow up in all aspects into Him."
- Second: "The whole body… according to the proper working of each individual part, causes the growth of the body."

Do you see this spiritual dynamic? I hope you do! The conclusion is clear. Immaturity in individual members of the Church causes stagnation of the spiritual growth of the entire body. And this is the greatest danger of spiritual immaturity.

I believe that five essential aspects derive from Ephesians 4:16. They are:

1. The whole body, being fitted together
2. The whole body, being held together
3. By what every joint supplies
4. Every individual part must contribute to the work of spiritual growth and maturity of the entire body, and
5. The body—the Church—is to be built on love.

Allow me to say a few things about each of these five aspects.

1. The whole body, being fitted together

This sounds good on paper, but the question is: what can accomplish the fitting together of the Body of Christ?

I think you'll agree that love binds the Body together. In his letter to the Colossians, Paul indicates that compassion, kindness, humility, gentleness, patience, and forgiveness are all important for the local church's overall spiritual and emotional health. Then he writes: "Beyond all these things put on love, which is the perfect bond of unity" (Colossians 3:14). You see? ***Love is the perfect bond of unity.***

We can only arrive at this profound point of understanding through a personal experience of the death and resurrection of Christ. The Bible teaches us:

> For the love of Christ *controls* and *urges* and *impels* us, because we are of the opinion and conviction that [if] One died for all, then all died; and He died for all, so that all those who live might live no longer to and for themselves, but to and for Him who died and was raised again for their sake. (2 Corinthians 5:14–15 AMP)

Only when we understand our identification in Christ's death and resurrection can we live for Him, not ourselves. There is no other cure for our self-centeredness than the cross of Christ. If we are to "grow up in all aspects into Him," we must practice speaking the truth in love. In other words, in our fellowship with one another, we must exercise enough transparency and acceptance to speak the truth, not in hurtful ways, but in love. John writes so tenderly: "Little children, let us not love with word or with tongue, but in deed and *truth*" (1 John 3:18). At the opening of his second letter, John writes: "Grace, mercy, and peace will be with us, from God the Father and from Jesus Christ, the Son of the Father, *in truth and love*" (2 John 1:3). Similarly, in the third letter, John writes: "The elder to the beloved Gaius, whom I *love in truth*" (3 John 3:1). *Agape love cannot exist without truth; and truth cannot exist without agape love.* These two go hand in hand and contribute to our spiritual growth.

2. The whole body being held together

This speaks of profound organic unity! But the question is: what keeps (or holds) the Body of Christ together?

The only thing that can accomplish this is *truth*. Truth is the only *force* that keeps the Christian Church together. Only the Person of Truth—*Christ Himself*—holds us together. Here is a powerful Scripture: "He is before all things, and in Him all things hold together" (Colossians 1:17). Christ, in a sense, is the *belt of truth* that wraps around us. Paul writes: "stand, therefore, having your loins *girded about with truth*, and having on the breastplate of righteousness" (Ephesians 6:14). "Having your loins girded about with truth," means "to encircle with a belt or band" and "to prepare (oneself) for action." In the Old Testament, it is written,

These words, which I am commanding you today, shall be on your heart. You shall teach them diligently to your sons and shall talk of them when you sit in your house and when you walk by the way and when you lie down and when you rise up. You shall **bind them** as a sign on your hand, and they shall be as frontals on your forehead. (Deuteronomy 6:6–8)

Commenting on this verse, John Wesley writes:

Thou shalt bind them—Thou shalt give all diligence, and use all means to keep them in thy remembrance, as men often bind something upon their hands, or put it before their eyes to prevent forgetfulness of a thing which they much desire to remember."[41]

In other words, we should behold the Lord Jesus and be constantly mindful of His words. The wise king of the Old Testament writes: "Bind them on your fingers; Write them on the tablet of your heart" (Proverbs 7:3).

3. By what every joint supply

We all agree that Christ has only one Church. He is coming for a single Bride, not for 43,000 *little brides*. The Body of Christ is not a member by itself but many members in unity! Still, practically speaking,

God's people live in much disunity. Paul understood the principle of organic unity very well. He writes: "For the body is not one member, but many" (1 Corinthians 12:14).

I challenge you to keep in mind the following principle: "What makes the physical body powerful is not the individual members separated from each other but rather the joints coming together in unity." The same is true in the spiritual arena. When believers are tightly bound with God and each other by obeying His commands, they can fight to advance His kingdom instead of quarreling with each other. The Bible promises: "How could one chase a thousand, and two put ten thousand to flight" (Deuteronomy 32:30a).

Allow me to illustrate. Let us look at the shoulder. The human shoulder is made up of three bones: the clavicle (collarbone), the scapula (shoulder blade), and the humerus (upper arm bone), as well as associated muscles, ligaments, and tendons. If any of these three bones were separate from each other, they could do nothing. What makes the shoulder powerful is that all these parts between the shoulder bones come together to make up the shoulder joints.

Let me give you another example: the elbow. The human elbow joint is the synovial hinge between the upper arm's humerus and the radius and ulna in the forearm, which allows the hand to be moved towards and away from the body. Obviously, these components (the humerus, the upper arm, and the radius and ulna) by themselves cannot perform (if separated from each other) what the elbow (as a joint) can do. Should I go further? Should I explain how the hip operates?

The hip joint, scientifically referred to as the acetabulofemoral joint, is the joint between the femur and acetabulum of the pelvis. Its primary function is to support the body's weight in static (standing) and dynamic (walking or running) postures. The hip joints are the most critical part of retaining balance. The pelvic inclination angle, the single most important element of human body posture, is adjusted at the hips. The coming together of the femur and acetabulum forms this important joint. These elements alone can do nothing, but together the hip joint helps the whole body when standing or running. Isn't this amazing? We could go on with these examples from the human body.

If these are true for the human body, it is the same for the spiritual Body—*the Church*. Paul writes: "For even as the body is one and yet has many members, and all the members of the body, though they are many, are one body, so also is Christ" (1 Corinthians 12:12). Think about a body that is decapitated! Can that body perform anything? Of course not! It does not function. It is dead.

In the same way, the spiritual body, *the Church,* cannot function. *The Church is dead without her perfect union with Christ.* That is why the Lord Jesus clearly tells his disciples, "Abide in Me, and I in you. As the branch cannot bear fruit of itself unless it abides in the vine, so neither can you unless you abide in Me"

(John 15:5). I hope we get this sooner rather than later.

3. Every individual part must contribute to the work of spiritual growth and maturity of the entire body

Now we reached the point where the rubber meets the road. In the same way that the three bones, the clavicle, the scapula, and the humerus, come together to form the joint of the shoulders, so it must be done in the body of Christ. The prophet Isaiah foretold about the coming of the Child who will be given to us. He stated, "the government will rest on His shoulders" (Isaiah 9:6). I don't think it would be stretch to say that Christ's "shoulders" on this earth are us—the Church, coming in unity to serve God's purposes. I like this connection! I hope you do too!

The Pareto principle, the law of the vital few, also known as the 20/80 Rule, states that: "for many events, roughly 80% of effects come from 20% of the causes."[42] This principle seems to affect churches as well. If we are sincere, we must attest to these facts:

- 20% of Christians complete 80% of the ministries of the local Church.
- 80% of financial contributions are donated by 20% of supporters.

Interesting, isn't it?

Moreover:

> According to researchers Scott Thumma and Warren Bird, most churches—mega-sized and small, black and white—are run by 20 percent of the congregation. The other 80 percent, they say, tend to act like spectators: they are minimally involved and attend infrequently or not at all.[43]

This is staggering! However, God does not want the 20/80 Rule to be in effect in His Church. God wants the 100/100 Rule to be in effect inside Christ's Body. The Bible tells us: "From whom the whole body, being fitted and held together by what every joint supplies, according to the proper working of each individual part, causes the growth of the body for the building up of itself in *love*" (Ephesians 4:16). In other words, there should be no idleness in the body of Christ.

No individual member should be "unemployed," but all should be involved in something good for God and others. Paul writes: "Now you are Christ's body, and individually members of it" (1 Corinthians 12:27). This has been written to discourage any forms of divisions inside the Body of Christ "so that there may be no division in the body, but *that* the members may have the same care for one another" (1 Corinthians 12:25).

4. The Body—the Church—is to be built on love

This, in a sense, is a climax in Paul's writings. He writes: "in whom the whole building, being fitted together, is growing into a holy temple in the Lord, in whom you also are being built together into a dwelling of God in the Spirit" (Ephesians 2:21–22). "According to the proper working of each individual part, causes the growth of the body for the building up of itself in love" (Ephesian 4:16b). I believe with all my heart that if every Christian were conscientious of this principle—the body of Christ is built on love—it would bring a tremendous revival. This would be a love revolution with every church member declaring: *Not me but Him. Not us but the Kingdom of God!*

No matter what, God will be consistent with His nature (agape love) and all His principles. Paul warns us, "Now if any man builds on the foundation with gold, silver, precious stones, wood, hay, straw, each man's work will become evident; for the day will show it because it is *to be* revealed with fire, and the fire itself will test the quality of each man's work" (1 Corinthians 3:12–13).

The more I investigate the vast theme of spiritual growth and maturity, the more I am convinced that as the individual members of any local church experience spiritual growth, *spiritual joints* are being formed by the Holy Spirit within the Universal Body. The Body of Christ reaches the point of "being fitted and held together." This is done by formation of joints. It is clear that the formation of the joints depends on "the proper working of each individual part." Do you see the chain of events? If Satan could keep most individual members of a local church disinterested in spiritual maturity, in a sense, he can prevent spiritual maturity in the entire local body. I have a suspicion that this is precisely the strategy the enemy uses.

That is why the Scripture is filled with the expressions "one another" and "each other." Before His crucifixion, in the most intimate setting (Holy Communion), Christ said:

> A new commandment I give to you, that you love one another, even as I have loved you, that you also love one another. By this all men will know that you are My disciples, if you have love for one another. (John 13:34-35)

As believers, we are called to:

- Be devoted to one another in love (Romans 12:10)
- Be of the same mind toward one another (Romans 12:16)
- Do not judge one another (Romans 14:13)
- Build up one another (Romans 14:19, 1 Thessalonians 5:11)
- Accept one another (Romans 15:7)
- Admonish one another (Romans 15:14;

Colossians 3:16)
- Greet one another with a sincere love (Rom. 16:16, 1 Peter 5:14)
- Display the same care for one another (1 Corinthians 12:25)
- Be kind to one another (Ephesians 4:32)
- Be tender-hearted, forgiving each other (Ephesians 4:32)
- Speak life to one another (Ephesians 5:19)
- Be subject to one another (Ephesians 5:21)
- Serve one another in love (Galatians 5:13)
- Bear one another's burdens (Galatians 6:2; Colossians 3:13)
- Display sincere understanding for one another (Ephesians 4:2)
- Regard one another as more important than yourselves (Philippians 2:3)
- Abound in love for one another and love each other (1 Thessalonians 3:12, 4:9; 2
- Thessalonians 1:3, 1 Peter. 1:22, 4:8; 1 John 3:11, 4:7, 4:11, 4:12; 2 John 1:5)
- Comfort one another (1 Thessalonians 4:18)
- Encourage one another (1 Thessalonians 5:11; Hebrew 3:13, 10:25)
- Live in peace with one another (1 Thessalonians 5:13)
- Seek good for one another (1 Thessalonians 5:15; Hebrews 10:24)
- Do not speak against one another (James

4:11)
- Do not complain against one another (James 5:9; 1 Peter 4:9)
- Confess your sins to one another (James 5:16)
- Pray for one another (James 5:16)
- Be hospitable to one another (1 Peter 4:9)
- Serve one another (1 Peter 4:10)
- Display genuine humility toward one another (1 Peter 5:5)

These are just a few references based only on the New Testament epistles. Imagine how long the list would be if we included the entire Bible.

Now is the best time to declare before God three positive things:

- God, I realized that up until now, I have just been a consumer in the Body of Christ.
- Dear Lord Jesus, please make me and mold me in such a way that I may fulfill my role and destiny in Your Spiritual Body.
- Holy Spirit, please reveal to me the place, the function, and the gift I have and, most importantly, where I belong in the Body of Christ. Make me part of that special joint that only I was created to fulfill.

Let's pray this prayer:

Father God, thank you for the gift I have in Christ. Now I am part of Your Eternal Family. I desire to be productive in the place you ordered me to be. My heart longs to be effective in the function You have given me. Lord Jesus, I want to be organically connected with you to produce much fruit for God's glory. Holy Spirit, please form and mold me into the spiritual joint I have been designed to be. My chief desire is that, together with the rest of the members of the Church, we may work in unity for one cause only. That is the Body of Christ, to shine so the whole universe will see Your great work. I pray in the wonderful name of Jesus. Amen!

Endnotes

[41] *John Wesley's Explanatory Notes*, Deuteronomy 6:6-8. www.christianity.com. Accessed on May 1, 2018. https://www.christianity.com/bible/commentary.php?com=wes&b=5&c=6.

[42] Olivia Guy-Evans, MSc, "The Pareto principle." Updated on September 21, 2023. www.simplypsychology.org. https://www.simplypsychology.org/pareto-principle.html

[43] Stephanie Samuel, "Churches' Dilemma: 80 Percent of Flock Is Inactive." Posted on Jun 26, 2011. www.christianpost.com. https://www.christianpost.com/news/authors-pastors-must-goafter-lost-sheep-to-increase-church-participation-51581/.

-6-

Spiritual Maturity:
Believers' Highest Priority

The last words of famous people still impact our lives today. Let me mention just a handful of them.

John Knox (1514-1572), a Scottish minister, Reformed Theologian, and the foremost leader of the Scottish Reformation, uttered these piercing words and then died: *"Live in Christ, die in Christ, and the flesh need not fear death."*[44]

Martin Luther (1483-1546), a German priest, theologian, author, and the seminal figure of the Protestant Reformation, said: *"Our God is the God from whom cometh salvation. God is the Lord by whom we escape death."*[45]

Richard Baxter, 17th Century Puritan Theologian, said: *"I have pain—but I have peace, I have peace."*[46]

Dwight Lyman Moody (1837-1899), the great evangelist of the late 19th Century, on his deathbed turned to his boys who were at his bedside and said: *"If God be your partner, make your plans large."*[47]

The list can continue, but I will stop here. Now, let us look at some of the famous words of known leaders from the Bible.

Among Moses' last words contain special encouragement to the children of Israel as they were preparing to go into the Promised Land-finally: "Be strong and courageous, do not be afraid or tremble at them, for the LORD your God is the one who goes with you. He will not fail you or forsake you" (Deuteronomy 31:6). Interestingly enough these words are carried over into the New Testament to be a great encouragement to us as well: "I WILL NEVER DESERT YOU, NOR WILL I EVER FORSAKE YOU" (Hebrews 13:5).

Joshua was the leader God used to bring Israel into the Promised Land. Among his last words are: "Now, therefore, fear the LORD and serve Him in sincerity and truth; and put away the gods which your fathers served beyond the River and in Egypt, and serve the LORD" (Joshua 24:14).

These are among King David's last words: "For all my salvation and all my desire, Will He not indeed make it grow?" (2 Samuel 23:4b).

Paul's last words are monumental! He writes:

> I solemnly charge you in the presence of God and of Christ Jesus, who is to judge the living and the dead, and by His appearing and His kingdom: preach the word; be ready in season

and out of season; reprove, rebuke, exhort, with great patience and instruction. For the time will come when they will not endure sound doctrine; but wanting to have their ears tickled, they will accumulate for themselves teachers in accordance to their own desires, and will turn away their ears from the truth and will turn aside to myths. (2 Timothy 4:1–4)

Sobering, isn't it? Personally, I like Saint Peter's last words very much. He writes:

You, therefore, beloved, knowing this beforehand, be on your guard so that you are not carried away by the error of unprincipled men and fall from your own steadfastness, but grow in the grace and knowledge of our Lord and Savior Jesus Christ. To Him be the glory, both now and to the day of eternity. Amen. (2 Peter 3:17-18)

I saved the best for last. Over and above all leaders is our Lord and Savior, Jesus Christ. Before He ascended to heaven, the Lord charged His disciples (and implicitly) all of us with these words:

Go therefore and make disciples of all the nations, baptizing them in the name of the Father and the Son and the Holy Spirit, teaching them to observe all that I commanded you; and lo, I am with you always, even to the end of the age. (Matthew 28:19-20)

These two verses are known as the Great Commission.[48] This is the vision and the mission of His Church.

I believe the entire Bible, from Genesis to Revelation, is the inspired Word of God. Paul writes:

> All Scripture is inspired by God and profitable for teaching, for reproof, for correction, for training in righteousness; so that the man of God may be adequate, equipped for every good work. (2 Timothy 3:16-17)

This means that, for every aspect of our lives and spiritual development, the Word of God has the solution, provides the guidance needed, and has something to say to us, even the power to rebuke us in His Love and Grace.

Since the Lord Jesus desires believers to be disciples and make disciples, and Saint Peter's last words are about spiritual growth, let us look at a few critical aspects for all believers.

1. Spiritual Growth Should be the Most Important Aspect for all Believers

After the salvation experience, when we accepted Jesus into our hearts by faith, the most critical aspect of believers' lives is the process of spiritual growth and maturity, or progressive sanctification.

In Chapter 3 of *Fullness of Christ,* titled "Spiritual Growth in Christ," I wrote:

> Spiritual growth is the work of God through His grace by which God's children are transformed according to the image of Christ in the inner self and are empowered to die to the false self and live in righteousness and holiness. [49]

As you can see, the Father desires us to be more like His Son.

2. The Process of Spiritual Growth and Maturity is Not a Function of Time

Many believers erroneously think they will grow and mature if they attend the local church, somehow on some automatic pilot. Spiritual growth is not a function of time; it is a function of:

A. Abiding
B. Surrender
C. Spiritual food

In other words, believers can attend the local church for 30 years but, spiritually speaking, be just a three-year-old toddler.

A. Abiding

In John 15, the Lord Jesus Christ explained to the disciples that He is the Vine, and God the Father is the Vinedresser.

Jesus specifically tells us to abide in Him. John writes:

> Abide in Me, and I in you. As the branch cannot bear fruit of itself unless it abides in the vine, so neither can you unless you abide in Me. I am the vine, you are the branches; he who abides in Me and I in him, he bears much fruit, for apart from Me you can do nothing. (John 15:4-5)

Based on these two verses, it is crystal clear that the only recipe for spiritual fruitfulness—is abiding in the true Vine, in other words, abiding in Christ.

The word abide means *to remain, to stay in position*, in other words, *to be continually connected with Christ*.

B. Surrender

In Romans 12:1 and 2, the apostle Paul tells believers:

> Therefore, I urge you, brethren, by the mercies of God, to present your bodies a living and holy sacrifice, acceptable to God, which is your

spiritual service of worship. And do not be conformed to this world, but be transformed by the renewing of your mind, so that you may prove what the will of God is, that which is good and acceptable and perfect. (Romans 12:1-2)

Since Romans 12 starts with *"therefore,"* we must pause and ask ourselves: What is this there for? In other words, Paul emphasizes everything he taught in his letter from Roman Chapter 1 to Roman Chapter 11 in Romans 12:1 and 2.[50] The very essence of these two verses, is that spiritual transformation is NOT possible without the mind renewal produced by the living word of God and by the power of the Holy Spirit.

In other words, the central focus of these two verses is spiritual transformation. Spiritual metamorphosis is NOT possible without renewal of the mind, produced by the living Word of God and the power of the Holy Spirit.

To move toward this spiritual transformation and mind renewal level, the believer must willingly offer everything- the will, body, soul, emotions, mind, and thoughts on God's altar.

C. Spiritual food

If we look carefully in the New Testament, especially in the letters of Paul, Peter, and John, we will soon discover that there are two major categories of spiritual food:

- Milk
- Solid food

The author of Hebrews, in chapter 5, verses 12 to 14, writes:

> For though by this time, you ought to be teachers, you have need again for someone to teach you the elementary principles of the oracles of God, and you have come to need milk and not solid food. For everyone who partakes only of milk is not accustomed to the word of righteousness, for he is an infant. But solid food is for the mature, who because of practice have their senses trained to discern good and evil. (Hebrews 5:12—14)

Very briefly, this critical passage communicates that if a believer consumes only the elementary principles/teachings of the Bible—considered milk diet, cannot develop spiritual discernment, "discern good and evil," and cannot consume solid food. The solid food diet teaches about righteousness, the finished work of the cross, the manifold aspects of God's grace, spiritual identity, spiritual warfare, and so on.

So, believers must transition from the "milk diet" to the "solid food diet."

Immediately after chapter 5, in chapter 6:1-2, the

Bible commands us:

> Therefore, leaving the elementary teaching about the Christ, let us press on to maturity, not laying again a foundation of repentance from dead works and of faith toward God, of instruction about washings and laying on of hands, and the resurrection of the dead and eternal judgment. (Hebrews 6:1—2)

"Let us press on to maturity" is not a suggestion; it is an instruction to be taken to heart and to be obeyed.

3. Becoming partakers of the divine nature

The second appeal of Saint Peter is magnificent. In chapter 1:2—4 of this letter, Peter writes:

> Grace and peace be multiplied to you in the knowledge of God and of Jesus our Lord; seeing that His divine power has granted to us everything pertaining to life and godliness, through the true knowledge of Him who called us by His own glory and excellence. For by these He has granted to us His precious and magnificent promises, so that by them you may become partakers of the divine nature, having escaped the corruption that is in the world by lust. (2 Peter 1:2—4)

As we look carefully into these three verses, let's consider these aspects:

- Growing in the knowledge of our Lord Jesus, multiplying the grace of God and His peace.
- The Divine Vine Dresser has granted us everything we need in our day-to-day living and for developing a godly character.

In other words, believers do not need anything else to live an abundant life that has not yet been granted to them.

If we ask for more power, God answers: *"I have already granted you all the power I have."* (See 2 Corinthians 4:7, Ephesians 3:20.)

If we ask Jesus for more of His presence in our lives, Christ reminds us: *"I have already given you the Holy Spirit to be with and in you."* See John 14:16 and 16:13. This divine Helper is always with us no matter what.

Some Bible scholars tell us that there are more than 7,000 promises in the Bible. The apostle Paul assures us that, in Christ, all those promises are Yes and Amen. The Bible tells us: "For as many as are the promises of God, in Him they are yes; therefore, also through Him is our Amen to the glory of God through us." (2 Corinthians 1:20)

Therefore, for Christ's disciples, there is no limit regarding their spiritual growth and transformation.

It is up to us as believers to walk in God's promises, abide in Christ, surrender our lives to God, start transitioning from the milk to the solid food diet, and become partakers of His divine nature. That is why the subtitle of my book, *Fullness of Christ,* is *"expressing God's nature and character in and through you."*

4. Climb the ladder of maturity

Saint Peter continues:

> Now for this very reason also, applying all diligence, in your faith supply moral excellence, and in your moral excellence, knowledge, and in your knowledge, self-control, and in your self-control, perseverance, and in your perseverance, godliness, and in your godliness, brotherly kindness, and in your brotherly kindness, love. (2 Peter 1:5—7)

I don't intend to unpack this critical Bible passage in this chapter. Peter makes it clear that it is up to us to apply all diligence (not 25%, not 50%, not 75%, not even 99.99%, but—100%—all diligence.) God supplied everything, that means 100%, pertaining to life and godliness. He is simply admonishing us to apply all diligence (100%). Applying all diligence has a tremendous result:

- Having the qualities in abundance

renders us fruitful.

Choosing not to apply all diligence leads to adverse outcomes:

- o Spiritual blindness
- o Spiritual myopia
- o Spiritual amnesia

Let us pay attention to the Word of God:

For if these qualities are yours and are increasing, they render you neither useless nor unfruitful in the true knowledge of our Lord Jesus Christ. For he who lacks these qualities is blind or short-sighted, having forgotten his purification from his former sins. (2 Peter 1:8–9)

The benefits of the diligent believers are fantastic:

- Benefit 1. Diligent believers never stumble.
- Benefit 2. Diligent believers have abundant access to the kingdom of God.

Let us listen carefully to what Saint Peter has to say:

Therefore, brethren, <u>be all the more diligent</u> to

make certain about His calling and choosing you; for as long as you practice these things, you will never stumble; for in this way the entrance into the eternal kingdom of our Lord and Savior Jesus Christ will be abundantly supplied to you. (2 Peter 1:10—11)

Dear brothers and sisters, beloved children of God, and disciples of Christ, I believe with all my heart that the Holy Spirit inspired me to write *Fullness of Christ: expressing God's Nature in Character in and through you,* to be a valuable TOOL that will HELP you tremendously in your process of spiritual growth and maturity.

The last verse I want to leave with you to close the circle entirely is from John chapter 15, verse 8: "My Father is glorified by this, that you bear much fruit, and so prove to be My disciples" (John 15:8).

Do you see this? Spiritual fruitfulness glorifies God. Therefore, spiritual growth and maturity is not for a selected few. The Father God desires all His beloved children to reach the level of fruitfulness to glorify Him and, through a series of decisions leading to total surrender, will lead to a purer worship of God.

May God richly bless you, my beloved!

Endnotes:

[44] Dennis Rainey, "Famous Last Words of Well-Known Christians." August 2023. www.christianity.com. Accessed on February 4, 2024. https://www.christianity.com/wiki/people/famous-last-words-11545269.html.

[45] "Famous Last Words of Well-Known Christians."

[46] Dennis Rainey.

[47] Ibid.

[48] For more details about the Great Commission please refer to my book, *"The Great Commission: A Closer Look at Why Discipleship Cannot Be Ignored."* Click on https://amzn.to/41OsRe1, to buy it on Amazon.

[49] Valy Vaduva, *Fullness of Christ,* (Upper Room Fellowship Ministry, Livonia, MI, 2018), 22. Click on https://amzn.to/3mTcDBp to buy it on Amazon.

[50] Disclosure: It will take many hours to unpack those significant verses, so I recommend reading/studying *Fullness of Christ.*

Reflection Questions:

Please reflect upon the following questions, briefly elaborate, then share your thoughts with a friend or with your small group.

1. What did the Holy Spirit whisper to your heart through this chapter? What did you like the most in chapters 1-5?

_____
_____
_____
_____

2. What new concepts did you learn from chapters 1-5? Which idea are you committed to implementing in your life?

_____
_____
_____
_____

3. From the five dangers the author discussed in the book, which danger do you consider the deadliest?

_____
_____
_____
_____

4. After a careful study of the five dangers, please write short summaries of each of them. If necessary, please use a separate piece of paper.

Danger 1: _____
_____
_____

Danger 2: _____
_____
_____

Danger 3: _____
_____
_____

Danger 4. _____
_____
_____

Dangers 5: _____
_____
_____

4.1. *Carnality.* Which aspects resonated in your own heart? In what areas did you sense the conviction of the Holy Spirit?

_____
_____
_____
_____
_____
_____
_____

4.2. *Instability.* Which aspects resonated in your own heart? In what areas did you sense the conviction of the Holy Spirit?

_____
_____
_____
_____
_____
_____
_____
_____
_____
_____
_____

4.3. *Repulsion towards Solid Food.* Which aspects resonated in your own heart? In what areas did you sense the conviction of the Holy Spirit?

_____
_____
_____
_____
_____
_____
_____
_____
_____
_____
_____

4.4. *Spiritual Identity Ignorance.* Which aspects resonated in your own heart? In what areas did you sense the conviction of the Holy Spirit?

_____
_____
_____
_____
_____
_____
_____
_____
_____
_____
_____

4.5. *Inability to Make a Meaningful Contribution to the Spiritual Body of Christ.* Which aspects resonated in your own heart? In what areas did you sense the conviction of the Holy Spirit?

_____
_____
_____
_____
_____
_____
_____
_____
_____
_____

5. After a careful reading/studying of *Spiritual Maturity: Believers' Highest Priority*:

5.1 What did the Holy Spirit whisper to your heart through this chapter? What did you like the most in this chapter?

_____
_____
_____
_____

5.2 What new concepts did you learn from this chapter? Which idea are you committed to implementing in your life?

_____
_____
_____
_____

6. List the best aha moments you had while reading this book.

_____
_____
_____
_____
_____
_____
_____
_____

Upper Room Fellowship Ministry

In 1996, in response to God's calling and with the guidance of the Holy Spirit, Upper Room Fellowship Ministry (URFM) was formed to serve the body of Christ. It is a non-profit and non-denominational Christian organization.

Upper Room
Fellowship Ministry

Vision
Fully alive through mind renewal and spiritual transformation for God's glory.

Mission

We desire to assist believers in experiencing healing for the wounded heart, restoration for the soul, and spiritual growth in Christ. Our prayer and deep desire are that you experience Jesus Christ as your very source of life through the Holy Spirit.

Through individual or small group meetings and retreats, our ministry is committed to creating an environment where healing, restoration, and spiritual freedom can be experienced. Under the guidance of the Holy Spirit, URFM is making disciples and equipping them for the Kingdom of God. This organization ministers to the spiritual growth of all believers.

The goal is that every member of Christ's Body would attain the Ultimate Intention—the fullness of Christ.

Most Christians have been taught that Jesus Christ died for their sins. Some embraced Christ as their Lord. Only a few have been taught the truth that they died with Him and experienced Christ as their Life. Consequently, even fewer find victory in their lives. Although they have been set free from their sins, they have not been set free from themselves.

Our desire and fervent prayer for all of Jesus' disciples are that they all will become everything that God intends for them to become, in other words—the fullness of Christ.

About the author

Valy Vaduva was born in Romania, a beautiful country in Eastern Europe. He became a follower of Jesus at sixteen and started preaching the Gospel at seventeen. He loves the Bible and takes the Great Commission very seriously. Valy is passionate about spiritual growth. His greatest desire is to see believers grow up in all aspects in Jesus, be transformed by the Holy Spirit, and reach the fullness of Christ. Therefore, he loves working with believers who desire to grow in the grace and knowledge of Christ. Valy is an ordained minister and the co-founder and president of the Upper Room Fellowship Ministry (URFM).

He earned his Master of Arts in Spiritual Formation and Leadership from Spring Arbor University.

As a certified Spiritual Life Coach, Valy offers personalized spiritual formation sessions in person and online. Valy and his wife, Elena, have four married children and ten grandchildren. They live in Michigan, USA.

www.ingramcontent.com/pod-product-compliance
Lightning Source LLC
Chambersburg PA
CBHW060340050426
42449CB00011B/2798